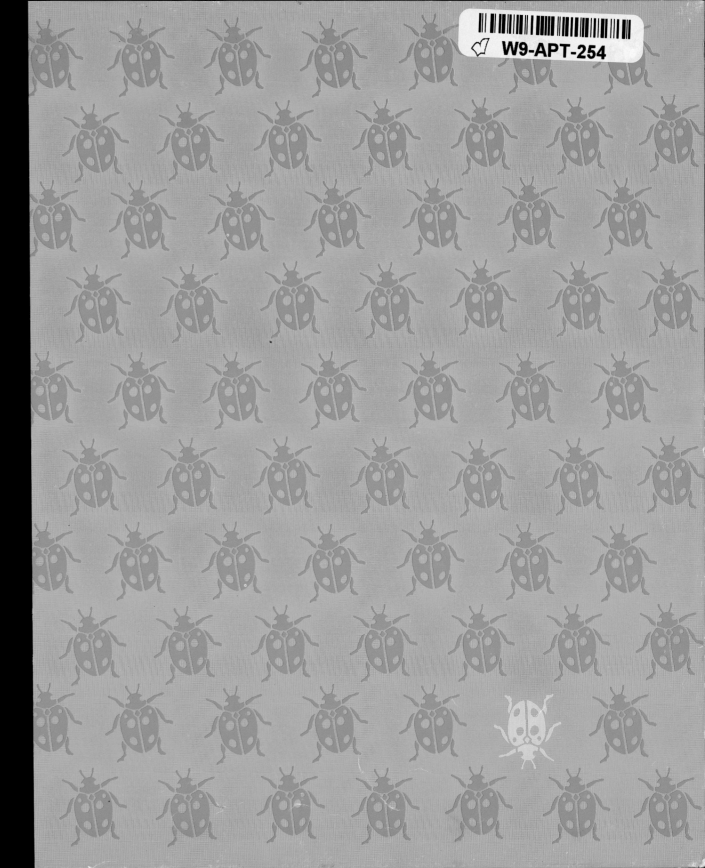

DK

A DORLING KINDERSLEY BOOK

Conceived, edited, and designed by DK Direct Limited

Note to parents

What's Inside? Insects is designed to help young children
understand the fascinating secrets of insects' bodies.
It illustrates what is inside a caterpillar, how a
spiny stick insect lays eggs, and why a fly is able to walk
on the ceiling. It is a book for you and your child
to read and talk about together, and to enjoy.

Designers   Sonia Whillock and Juliette Norsworthy
Typographic Designer   Nigel Coath
US Editor   B. Alison Weir
Editor   Sarah Phillips
Design Director   Ed Day
Editorial Director   Jonathan Reed

Illustrator   Richard Manning
Photographer   Frank Greenaway
Writer   Angela Royston

Insects supplied by the Natural History Museum, London,
and Trevor Smith's Animal World

First American Edition, 1992

SCHOLASTIC BOOK CLUB EDITION
•
Dorling Kindersley, Inc., 232 Madison Avenue
New York, New York 10016

Library of Congress Catalog Card Number: 91-58215

ISBN 0-590-46615-1

Printed in Italy

WHAT'S INSIDE?

INSECTS

DK

DORLING KINDERSLEY, INC.
NEW YORK

BEETLE

This is a snout beetle. It is called this because of its big, funny "nose." Its jaws are at the end and it uses them to eat plants.

Like all insects, the beetle has six legs. They have joints like our knees and elbows.

Here are the beetle's eyes.

Here are the beetle's antennae.

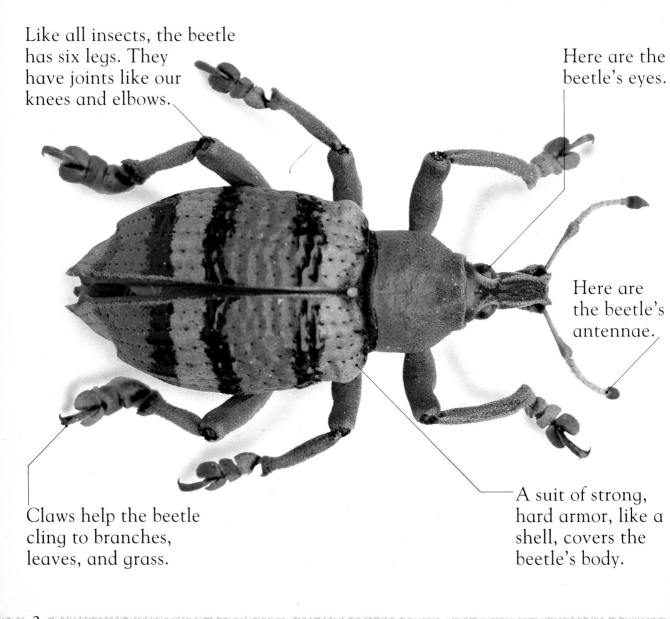

Claws help the beetle cling to branches, leaves, and grass.

A suit of strong, hard armor, like a shell, covers the beetle's body.

A beetle is an insect. Like all insects, its body has three parts: a head, a middle part, called the thorax, and a back end, called the abdomen.

Inside the beetle's hard shell, its body is soft. All parts of the body need blood, to bring food and take away waste.

This is the beetle's brain.

A beetle's heart is a long tube. From it, blood goes to all parts of the body.

HONEYBEE

This honeybee lives in a hive with many other bees. It feeds on pollen and nectar which it collects from flowers. Both pollen and nectar are stored inside the hive, where the nectar is made into honey.

Black and yellow stripes warn birds and other animals that bees have a poisonous sting.

The bee sucks up sweet nectar with its long tongue.

The honeybee's body is covered with hair. Pollen sticks to the hairs as the bee pushes into the center of the flower.

Inside the hive are lots of rooms, where the honey and pollen are stored.

Poison for the bee's stinger is made here. It is the poison that makes the sting hurt.

This is the bee's honey stomach. It stores the nectar here until it takes it back to the hive.

This is the bee's stinger. It only stings once and dies soon after.

The honeybee uses the hairs on its back legs to comb the pollen into this bag.

CATERPILLAR

Like all insects, this caterpillar hatched out of an egg. Now it lives on leaves and spends most of its time eating. It is growing fast. Soon it will begin to change into a butterfly.

The caterpillar breathes through these holes along its sides. They are called spiracles.

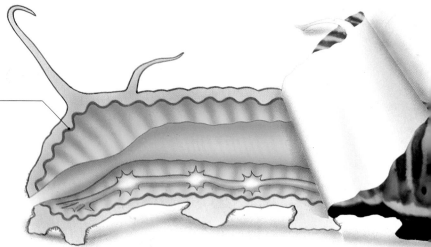

As it grows, a caterpillar gets too big for its skin. First a new, larger skin grows underneath, then the old skin splits and the caterpillar crawls out and leaves it behind.

Birds leave this caterpillar alone. Its bright colors and tentacles trick them into thinking it's poisonous.

The caterpillar holds food with its front three pairs of legs. The other legs are for walking and holding on to leaves.

This is the caterpillar's food tube. It is very big because the caterpillar eats so much.

Nerves from here spread all over its body, so that the caterpillar can feel things around it.

FLY

Have you ever wanted to walk on the ceiling like a fly? You would have to have a fly's sticky feet to do so. Many people kill flies because they spread germs.

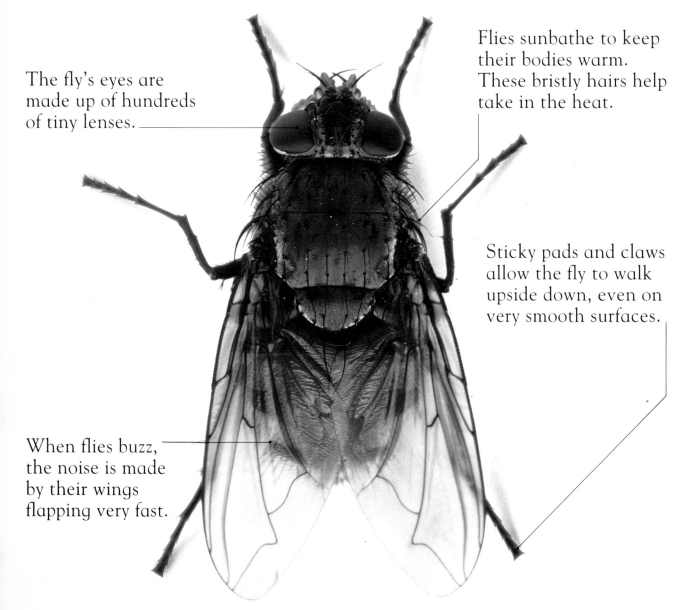

The fly's eyes are made up of hundreds of tiny lenses.

Flies sunbathe to keep their bodies warm. These bristly hairs help take in the heat.

Sticky pads and claws allow the fly to walk upside down, even on very smooth surfaces.

When flies buzz, the noise is made by their wings flapping very fast.

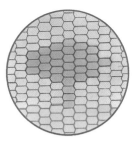

When a fly looks at something, it sees it broken up into lots and lots of little pieces, like a mosaic.

The fly breathes in and out through holes in its sides, called spiracles.

These are the fly's air sacs. They carry air to all parts of the body.

This fly, like some other insects, can taste with its feet.

CRICKET

This bush cricket lives in rough, grassy places.
It comes out in the evening and eats plants.
If it senses danger, it will quickly hop away.

This cricket is green, just like grass, which helps it hide from birds that would like to eat it.

Long antennae tell the cricket what the things around it feel and smell like.

Crickets use their long back legs to leap away from danger.

Crickets have "ears" on their front legs.

This strong muscle
straightens the back
leg as the cricket leaps.

Strong cords in the
legs, called tendons,
help the cricket
leap a long way.

These are the
ovaries. They
produce eggs,
from which baby
crickets grow.

This muscle is
used to bend the
leg back up again.

LADYBUG

Ladybugs are a kind of beetle. They live in forests, fields, parks, and gardens. Gardeners like ladybugs because they eat the aphids (small insects) that feed on garden plants.

Not all ladybugs have spots like this one. Some have stripes!

Ladybugs are brightly colored to warn birds and other animals that they taste bad.

The ladybug's hard back is really a pair of wings. They make a strong shield to keep the ladybug safe.

When a ladybug wants to fly, its hard front wings swing out to the sides. The hard wings do not flap, but they help lift the ladybug into the air.

Underneath the ladybug's hard back there are lots of nerves. They help the ladybug feel the things around it.

This is the ladybug's brain.

Nerves go all the way down the ladybug's legs. Others go to the tips of its antennae.

These nerves are like telephone wires. They carry messages around the body.

BUTTERFLY

This butterfly is called a lime swallowtail. It flits from flower to flower, sipping the nectar. Its wings are brightly colored, so birds peck at them instead of the butterfly's head and body.

When the butterfly feeds, it uncurls this long tube and uses it like a straw to suck up the flower's sweet nectar.

Butterflies taste with their feet.

When the butterfly is resting, it folds its wings above its back.

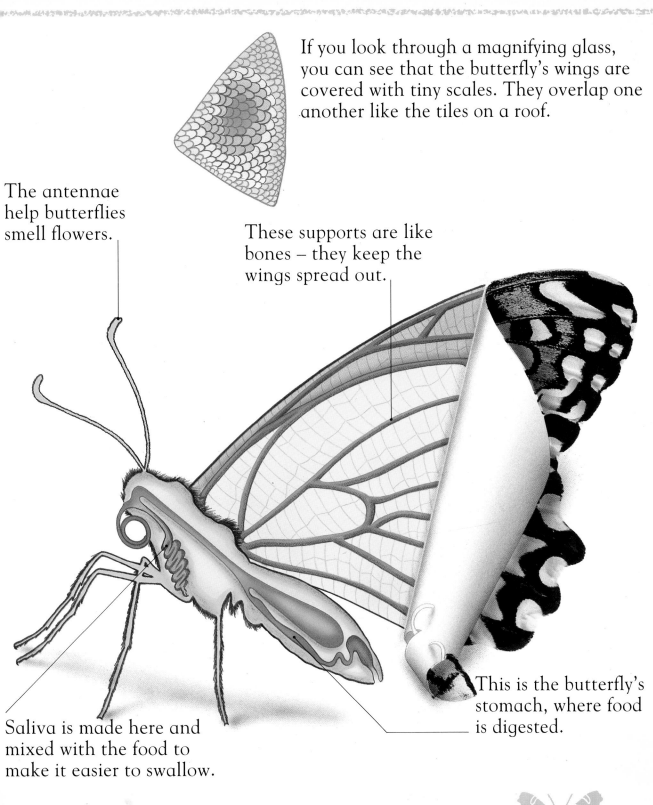

If you look through a magnifying glass, you can see that the butterfly's wings are covered with tiny scales. They overlap one another like the tiles on a roof.

The antennae help butterflies smell flowers.

These supports are like bones – they keep the wings spread out.

This is the butterfly's stomach, where food is digested.

Saliva is made here and mixed with the food to make it easier to swallow.

STICK INSECT

If you saw this spiny stick insect on a tree, you might think it was just a dried-up leaf. A stick insect moves slowly and sways as it walks, so that it looks like part of the tree moving in the wind. The insect cannot fly away from danger, but has other ways of defending itself.

The stick insect curls its body over its back to look like a scorpion with a stinging tail. Any enemy who does see it will keep far away.

Its legs look like dry leaves.

The body is brownish yellow Birds and lizards cannot see the stick insect among the twigs and leaves.

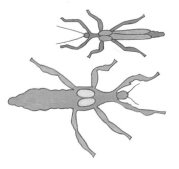

The female spiny stick insect is much bigger than the male.

In female stick insects, ovaries produce the eggs. The eggs travel down to the opening at the end of the tail.

The eggs come out here.

These muscles bunch up to bend its body around.